The Nature Kid's Guide to
WEASELS

DAVID ANDERSON

LP Media Inc. Publishing
Text copyright © 2026 by LP Media Inc.
All rights reserved.

For information address LP Media Inc. Publishing,
30012 Variolite St NW, Princeton MN 55371
www.lpmedia.org

Publication Data

Weasels
The Nature Kid's Guide to Weasels — First edition.

Summary: "Learn all about Weasels, the Nature Kid Way"
— Provided by publisher.

ISBN: 979-8-89818-159-8

[1. Weasels – Non-Fiction] I. Title.

Title: The Nature Kid's Guide to Weasels

CONTENTS

WILD WOODLANDS

DID YOU KNOW?

Weasels do not dig their own homes. They usually move into **burrows** left by mice and voles.

Crack! A weasel ducks beneath the shadows of a fallen branch.

Weasels can live almost anywhere, but they all need one thing — plenty of places to hide. Thick bushes, fallen logs, and rock piles are perfect. Some weasels live in cold snowy places, others in mild woodlands, and some in open meadows.

Wherever they live, weasels look for spots with small tunnels and holes nearby. Their long, slim bodies were built to follow prey underground.

Living near streams and ponds is a bonus. Water draws in mice and voles — and that means a steady supply of meals.

WEASELS WORLDWIDE

Weasels do not live in Australia. Stoats were brought there once but didn't survive.

Splash! A weasel darts across a shallow stream in a Swedish forest, searching for its next meal.

Weasels are found across a huge stretch of the world. They live in North America, Europe, Asia, and parts of North Africa. No other carnivore their size covers so much ground.

Least weasels range from Alaska and Canada all the way to Russia and Scandinavia. Long-tailed weasels roam the United States and down into Mexico.

Stoats — a close weasel cousin also known as the short-tailed weasel — are found across northern Europe and even in parts of Japan.

TINY TERRORS

It sounds impossible, but a weasel is able to fit its entire body through a hole the size of a wedding ring!

Click! Sharp claws tap the rocks. A hungry weasel hunts.

The least weasel holds a remarkable title — it is the smallest carnivore in the entire world. It weighs less than two slices of bread and is shorter than a new pencil. Something that fierce in such a tiny package is hard to believe.

Long-tailed weasels are bigger, growing up to about 16 inches. Even so, the largest weasels weigh less than a pound.

A hamster can outweigh the smallest weasels. But don't let the size fool you — these little hunters are anything but harmless.

SLINKY SHAPES

A weasel's spine has more bones than a human spine. This makes them super bendy!

Jump! A weasel bounds across the frozen ground.

A weasel's long, tube-shaped body is one of nature's most clever designs. It lets them slide into burrows and follow mice right into their own homes. No other predator can do that.

Most weasels wear thick brown fur with a cream or white belly. Their short, rounded ears lie flat against their head — another feature that helps them move through tight spaces.

With 34 needle-sharp teeth capable of crunching through bone and a highly flexible spine, a weasel is built from snout to tail to hunt.

SUPER SNIFFERS

A weasel can smell a mouse nest buried under several feet of snow — and will dive headfirst into the snowpack to reach it!

Sniff! The weasel catches the scent of prey on the breeze.

A weasel's most powerful tool is its nose. Smell is its primary sense for hunting — they can detect mice moving through tunnels underground and follow scent trails to track exactly where prey has been.

Their hearing is just as impressive. Weasels can detect high-pitched sounds far beyond what humans can hear, making them alert to the faintest rustle.

Eyesight is their weakest sense, but weasels still use their eyes to spot moving prey. When all three senses combine, very little escapes them.

STINKY SPRAY

Weasel musk smells a bit like skunk spray but is not as strong or long-lasting.

14

Snort! The weasel lifts its tail and sprays. It smells terrible!

Weasels carry a hidden defense near their tail — special glands that produce a powerfully smelly liquid called **musk**. When a weasel feels threatened, it releases this foul odor, and the smell is often enough to send a predator running in the other direction.

But musk is not just for defense. Weasels also rub and drag their bodies along surfaces to leave scent marks on their **territory**. Other weasels pick up the message quickly — this space is already claimed.

MEAT
MUNCHERS
16

Yawn! A weasel opens its mouth and shows off its sharp teeth!

Weasels are **carnivores** — they eat only meat, and they eat a lot of it. Mice and voles are their favorites, but a hungry weasel will also take rabbits, birds, eggs, frogs, and insects. They will eat almost anything that moves.

A weasel eats about half its body weight every single day. Their bodies burn through energy so fast that missing a meal is not an option. They must hunt often just to keep going.

Weasels sometimes store extra mice in their dens to eat later!

TUNNEL TAKEDOWN

Climb! A weasel climbs a pile of logs looking for a tunnel to search.

Weasels are the world's best tunnel hunters. Their bodies can fit through a hole barely an inch wide, letting them follow prey into spaces no other predator can reach.

Underground, they twist and turn through dark passages, tracking by smell until the chase ends. Above ground, they creep silently through tall grass, then pounce with lightning speed when prey is close.

A weasel is brave enough to take on a rabbit up to ten times its own size. That is a big target for such a small hunter.

WATCH OUT

DID YOU KNOW?
Weasels always fight back when attacked! They sometimes bite predators on the nose then dash away!

Crack! A branch breaks. The weasel runs to hide.

Weasels face danger from every direction. Hawks and owls are the biggest threats. These birds have sharp eyes and can spot a weasel from high in the sky. Great horned owls are especially dangerous because they hunt in the dark.

On the ground, foxes, coyotes, and even house cats will chase a weasel. Snakes are a different kind of threat — slim enough to follow a weasel right into its own burrow.

With so many hunters around, weasels must stay alert all day long.

QUICK ESCAPE

Weasels sometimes perform a wild spinning and jumping dance that confuses prey and predators alike, leaving them distracted long enough to escape!

Hoot! A weasel hears an owl and hides behind a fence post.

When danger comes, a weasel's first move is to disappear. Their slim bodies let them slip into spaces where nothing bigger can follow. They can vanish in seconds.

When running, weasels zigzag back and forth to confuse anything chasing them. They can also climb trees quickly to get off the ground in a hurry.

Rock piles, log stacks, and hollow stumps all make good hiding spots. A weasel always seems to know where the nearest escape is.

ZIP ZAP
DID YOU KNOW?
Weasels can turn around inside a tunnel without backing up. They just twist their flexible spine!
24

Zoom! A weasel darts through dry twigs. Its tiny body vanishes in a flash.

Weasels are fast runners. They can reach speeds of up to 15 miles per hour. Their short legs move in a blur.

When weasels run at full speed, they bound — pushing off with their back feet and landing on their front feet. Their body loops up and down with every jump, like a furry spring.

Weasels also swim well and can paddle across streams to chase prey. They can even dive underwater — like tiny, fierce otters.

BUSY BODIES

Some weasels travel over three miles in a single night just looking for food!

Bounce! A weasel bounds through the grass, searching for prey.

Weasels are active both day and night. Their bodies burn energy so fast that they may need to hunt up to ten times in a single day just to stay fed.

Between hunts, they take short naps in cozy dens hidden in old burrows, hollow logs, or under tree roots. Then they are back out again, covering their home range and looking for the next meal.

For a weasel, there is no such thing as a slow day.

LONE RANGERS

Crack! A weasel creeps through dry leaves. It hunts all alone.

Weasels live entirely on their own. They do not form packs, share dens, or travel together. Each weasel picks out a home range and guards it from other weasels.

Males have bigger home ranges than females — sometimes three or four times the size. Both use scent to let others know the area is taken.

The only time weasels look for each other is during mating season. After that, they go right back to living alone.

FINDING MATES

Trill! A male weasel calls out. It is early spring. He wants to find a mate.

Weasels mate in spring and summer. Males find females by following scent trails, sometimes traveling over a mile in a single night. They make a soft trilling sound when they find a mate.

After mating, female weasels have a special trick. Their bodies wait many months before the babies start growing. This way, kits are born in spring when there is plenty of food around.

KITS ARRIVE

Kits grow fast. They double their weight in just one week! By eight weeks old, they can hunt on their own.

Snuggle! A mother weasel curls around her newborn kits.

Baby weasels are called kits. A mother usually has four to eight at once, though some litters can reach twelve.

Newborns are very small — they weigh less than a nickel. Their eyes stay closed for about five weeks. They are born with no fur at all, just pink skin. After four days, a soft white fuzz begins to grow in.

At birth, kits cannot see or hear. They need their mother for everything.

MOM KNOWS

DID YOU KNOW?
Mother weasels move their kits if the nest feels unsafe!

Cute! A weasel mom watches over her babies closely.

Mother weasels raise kits alone. Fathers do not help, so the mother does all the feeding and teaching.

Kits drink their mother's milk for about five weeks. Then she brings them dead prey to eat. Soon she brings live prey so they can practice hunting.

Young weasels learn fast by watching their mother. They follow her on hunts around six weeks old. Kits leave home at about three months old. Then they must find their own territory to survive.

WINNING WAYS

Whoosh! A clever weasel darts through golden hay. It hunts for mice.

Weasels have been on Earth for a very long time. Old bones found in rock show that animals very much like today's weasels were living here long before most animals we know.

Their secret is simple. They can go where bigger hunters cannot. Forests, fields, farms, and meadows all work for them. Their small size lets them hunt in tunnels and tight spaces that no fox or hawk can reach.

SPOT ONE
FUN FACT!
Weasels are curious animals. They sometimes pop up to look at quiet watchers!
38

Peek! A weasel hears a soft noise and stands up to look around.

Weasels are some of the hardest wild animals to spot. They move fast, hide well, and most sightings last barely a second.

Look near stone walls, old logs, and field edges. These are spots weasels love to hunt. Early morning and evening are the best times to look.

Stay still and be quiet. Weasels are bold and curious. If you wait long enough without moving, you just might get a real look at one.

GLOSSARY

carnivore
An animal that eats only meat

musk
A smelly liquid that some animals make to protect themselves.

burrows
Holes or tunnels in the ground where animals live.

territory
An area that an animal claims as its own space.

camouflage
Colors or patterns that help an animal hide by blending in.